Dear Parent:
Your child's love of reading starts here!

Every child learns to read in a different way and at his or her own speed. Some go back and forth between reading levels and read favorite books again and again. Others read through each level in order. You can help your young reader improve and become more confident by encouraging his or her own interests and abilities. From books your child reads with you to the first books he or she reads alone, there are I Can Read Books for every stage of reading:

SHARED READING
Basic language, word repetition, and whimsical illustrations, ideal for sharing with your emergent reader

BEGINNING READING
Short sentences, familiar words, and simple concepts for children eager to read on their own

READING WITH HELP
Engaging stories, longer sentences, and language play for developing readers

READING ALONE
Complex plots, challenging vocabulary, and high-interest topics for the independent reader

ADVANCED READING
Short paragraphs, chapters, and exciting themes for the perfect bridge to chapter books

I Can Read Books have introduced children to the joy of reading since 1957. Featuring award-winning authors and illustrators and a fabulous cast of beloved characters, I Can Read Books set the standard for beginning readers.

A lifetime of discovery begins with the magical words **"I Can Read!"**

Visit www.icanread.com for information
on enriching your child's reading experience.

Dedicated to hardworking "mother bears"
all over the world.
—J.B.

The National Wildlife Federation & Ranger Rick contributors: Children's
Publication Staff, Licensing Staff, and in-house naturalist David Mizejewski

Ranger Rick: I Wish I Was a Polar Bear
Copyright © 2018 National Wildlife Federation. All rights reserved.
Manufactured in China. No part of this book may be used or reproduced in any manner whatsoever without
written permission except in the case of brief quotations embodied in critical articles and reviews. For
information address HarperCollins Children's Books, a division of HarperCollins Publishers, 195 Broadway,
New York, NY 10007.
www.icanread.com
www.RangerRick.com

Library of Congress Control Number: 2018934061
ISBN 978-0-06-243217-9 (trade bdg.) — ISBN 978-0-06-243216-2 (pbk.)

Book design by Celeste Knudsen

18 19 20 21 22 SCP 10 9 8 7 6 5 4 3 2 1 ❖ First Edition

I Can Read!

BEGINNING 1 READING

Ranger Rick®

I Wish I Was a Polar Bear

by Jennifer Bové

HARPER

An Imprint of HarperCollinsPublishers

What if you wished you were

a polar bear?

Then you became a polar bear cub.

Could you eat like a polar bear?

Play like a polar bear?

Grow up with a polar bear mom?

And would you want to? Find out!

Where would you live?

Polar bears live near the North Pole in a region called the Arctic. The Arctic is a cold, dry place.

Arctic land has very few trees.

It is called tundra.

The sea is frozen most of the year.

Would you like to live in a land with lots of ice?

7

What would your family be like?

Polar bear families are small.

Most families have one mother bear and two cubs.

Fathers and other polar bears
do not live with a family.
Adult polar bears spend
most of their time alone.

A mother polar bear

digs a den in the snow.

She crawls inside to give birth.

Falling snow covers the den opening.

Newborn cubs cuddle with their mom.

They drink her milk and grow bigger.

In the spring, the mother bear digs

a hole out of the deep snow.

The cubs see the snowy Arctic
for the first time.
It's time to explore
and learn to be a polar bear.

Do you ever explore
your neighborhood?

How would you learn to be a cub?

Like other young animals,

polar bear cubs learn by playing.

Wrestling helps them learn

to protect themselves

and their food from other bears.

Polar bears have no enemies except other polar bears. Cubs must learn to fight in case they need to defend themselves.

Polar bear cubs also learn
by watching their mother.
They copy everything she does.

Cubs follow their mother
when she hunts.
The cubs learn to swim
by hopping in and out
of the icy sea like their mom.

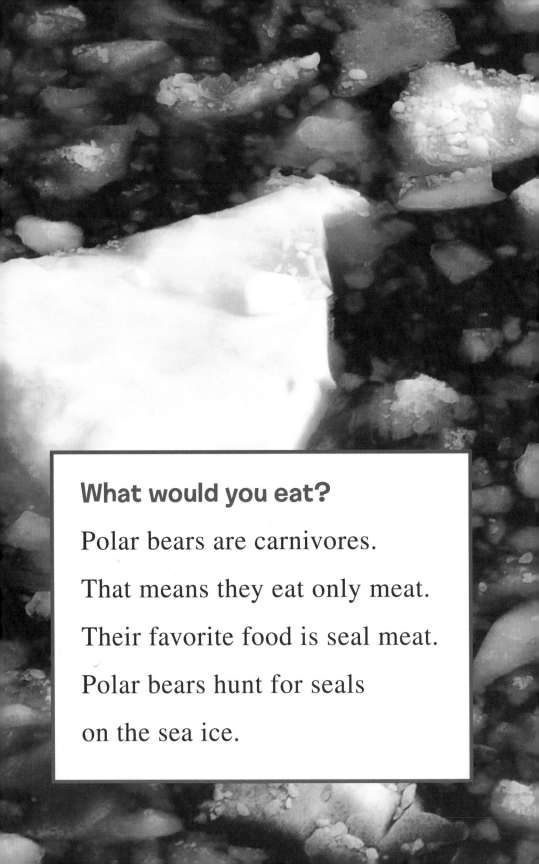

What would you eat?

Polar bears are carnivores.

That means they eat only meat.

Their favorite food is seal meat.

Polar bears hunt for seals

on the sea ice.

How would you talk?

Polar bears are usually quiet.

They touch noses to say "Hi."

Cubs wag their heads from side to side

to say "Let's play!"

When a polar bear is upset,
it may growl, roar, or chuff.
A chuff is a loud puff of breath
to say "Stay away!"

Where would you sleep?

Polar bears nap often,
but they don't have beds.
Sleepy polar bears lie down
on the cold snow to snooze.

Would you want to nap on the snow?

How would growing up change you?

Polar bears stay with their mother
for about three years.
By then, they've become big bears.
They are ready to leave their mom
and live on their own.

Adult bears live by themselves.

They travel, hunt, and sleep alone.

They aren't lonely, though.

A quiet life in the Arctic

is perfect for a polar bear.

Being a polar bear could be cool.

In fact, it would be cold!

Do you want to live in the Arctic?

Eat seal meat?

Dive into icy water?

Luckily, you don't have to.

You're not a polar bear.

You're YOU!

Did You Know?

- Polar bears are great swimmers. The longest polar bear swim on record was 426 miles (685 km).

- Polar bear cubs weigh about a pound at birth. Adult polar bears can weigh more than 1,000 pounds (453 kg). Polar bears are the largest land carnivores on earth.

- Adult polar bears have nearly five inches (12.7 cm) of fat under their skin. This special layer of fat is called blubber. The blubber keeps polar bears warm in one of the coldest places on earth.

Fun Zone

How does a thick layer of fat help polar bears stay warm? Try making a blubber glove to find out.

What You Need:
- 1 large bowl
- 1 tray of ice cubes
- 2 gallon-size plastic bags
- 2 cups vegetable shortening
- cold water

What You Do:
1. Place ice in the bowl.
2. Fill the bowl with cold water.
3. Scoop the shortening into one of the plastic bags.
4. Place your hand in the other plastic bag.
5. Now slide your plastic-covered hand into the bag with the shortening.
6. Smoosh the shortening around until it forms a layer all around your plastic-covered hand. The shortening, which is a vegetable fat, will act like a layer of blubber around your hand.
7. Put both of your hands into the bowl of icy water. Be careful not to let the water get into your plastic bags.

Notice that your hand inside the blubber glove is not as cold as your bare hand. This is because a layer of fat helps keep your body warm. A polar bear has blubber all over its body, plus a thick coat of fur, to survive in the Arctic cold.

Wild Words

Arctic: a region of land and sea surrounding the North Pole

Blubber: a thick layer of fat beneath a polar bear's skin

Carnivore: an animal that eats meat

Chuff: a loud puff of breath that polar bears make when they are upset

Den: a hole in the snow where a mother polar bear gives birth to cubs

North Pole: the point farthest north on Earth

Polar bear: the world's largest bear; lives in the Arctic

Seal: a sea mammal that is the polar bear's main food

Tundra: treeless land in the Arctic

Dig Deeper
WANT TO FIND OUT EVEN MORE ABOUT POLAR BEARS?

Check out the Ranger Rick website: www.RangerRick.com
SEARCH: polar bear